EXPLO**RING**

GREENLAND

Experience the Untamed Beauty and Fascinating Culture of Greenland

The Citi-scaper

The Citi-scaper Travel Guide

Table of Contents

INTRODUCTION

Do you want a journey that will take you to the very end of the globe and beyond? So pack your bags and go with us to Greenland, where the glaciers sing a symphony of utter amazement and the northern lights dance in the sky.

This travel guide will take you on a tour across the glaciers, tundras, and ice fjords of this far-flung and enigmatic region, taking you right into the heart of the Arctic.

A region unlike any other, Greenland is where the untamed wildness and unadulterated beauty of nature meet in a spectacular show of strength and grandeur. This book will lead you on an incredible tour through the most magnificent and thrilling locations in Greenland, regardless of your level of travel experience.

We will acquaint you with the inhabitants, their habits, and the marvels of this magnificent place, from the busy metropolis of Nuuk to the serene glaciers of Disko Bay.

Come join us and allow us to show you the wonders of Greenland, where you can go on fjord kayaking adventures, stroll across tundra, and watch the northern lights dance in the night sky. Prepare yourself for the experience of a lifetime as you explore this extraordinary location and learn about its hidden treasures and mysteries.

CHAPTER 1

OVERVIEW OF GREENLAND

Overview

The biggest island in the world, Greenland, is situated in the northern hemisphere, halfway between the Atlantic and Arctic Oceans. With a population of around 56,000, it is a separate territory inside the Kingdom of Denmark. Speaking both Danish and Kalaallisut's original tongue, the bulk of people reside in coastal locations.

The breathtaking landscapes of Greenland, which include glaciers, fjords, and mountains, are well recognized. Many animals, including polar bears, whales, and seals, call it home. Tourists flock to the nation to enjoy its distinctive landscapes and rich culture because of its natural beauty.

Fishing, hunting, and tourism are just a few of the natural resources that are vital to Greenland's economy.

A significant majority of the population is employed by the fishing sector, which is the greatest contributor to the economy. The nation is also making an effort to grow its mining and tourism sectors, both of which have the potential to bring about long-term economic gains.

The government of Greenland is making investments in the growth of renewable energy and other businesses despite its reliance on natural resources in order to diversify its economy and lessen its dependency on a single industry. This will support the nation's long-term economic development and stability.

In general, Greenland is a special place where travelers may enjoy its breathtaking scenery, rich culture, and dynamic economy. Greenland is a must-see location whether your interests lie in experiencing the nation's natural beauty, discovering its history and culture, or just taking in its diverse fauna.

The island country of Greenland is stunningly gorgeous. It is the biggest island in the world and the nation with the least amount of population, making it the ideal location for tourists looking for adventure, tranquility, and seclusion.

History

Greenland's history may be dated back to the nearly 4,500-year arrival of the first Inuit people. They were adept hunters and fishers who created a sophisticated civilization and way of life that was suitable for the harsh Arctic climate.

The Inuit depended on hunting and fishing to survive, and their resourcefulness and fortitude enabled them to prosper in the harsh Arctic environment.

The first European colony in Greenland was founded by the Viking Erik the Red in the latter part of the tenth century. The Vikings established a vibrant culture while residing in

Greenland for many centuries, trading with other northern settlements and going on raiding excursions.

The extreme environment provided problems, yet the Vikings were able to keep their colonies in Greenland for many years. Nevertheless, the Vikings ultimately abandoned their homes and headed back to Scandinavia as a result of the changing environment and diminishing supplies.

The return of European whalers and explorers to Greenland in the late 18th and early 19th centuries sparked a period of significant interaction between the Inuit and Western cultures.

Notwithstanding the difficulties the Inuit had as a consequence of this interaction, they managed to preserve their own cultural practices and continued to flourish in their Arctic homeland. This was partly because the Inuit people, whose culture was firmly established in the land and water of the Arctic, were resilient and strong.

International expeditions visited Greenland to examine its geology, climate, and fauna throughout most of the 20th century, and it remained a key hub of Arctic exploration and research. Greenland joined the Kingdom of Denmark in 1953 and attained independence in 1979.

Modern-day Greenland is a prosperous country with a strong Inuit culture, as well as booming fishing and tourist sectors.

The remnants of Viking cities, Inuit communities, and research stations are just a few of the intriguing historical monuments and museums open to tourists in Greenland. These locations provide visitors a rare chance to learn about the Inuit and Viking cultures that once inhabited Greenland and provide a window into the rich and interesting history of the Arctic.

This nation is certain to make an effect on everyone who visits, whether you are interested in learning about the history of the Arctic, experiencing the vibrant Inuit culture, or just appreciating the breathtaking natural beauty of Greenland.

Geography and Climate

Geography

Size and Location: Greenland covers an area of approximately 2.2 million square kilometers, making it the world's largest non-continental island. It is located between the Arctic and Atlantic Oceans, northeast of North America, and is geographically part of the continent of North America.

Landscapes: Greenland is predominantly covered by ice and glaciers, with the Greenland Ice Sheet being one of the largest ice masses in the world. The coastline is characterized by fjords, cliffs, and rocky shores. There are also mountains, including the highest peak, Gunnbjørn Fjeld, which reaches an elevation of 3,694 meters (12,119 feet).

Vegetation: Due to the Arctic climate, Greenland's vegetation is limited to hardy plants, mosses, and lichens. However, during the short summer months, colorful flowers and shrubs can be found in some regions, particularly in the southern parts.

Climate

Arctic Climate: Greenland experiences an Arctic climate, characterized by long, cold winters and short, cool summers. The climate is influenced by the cold waters of the surrounding oceans and the presence of ice and glaciers.

Temperature: Average temperatures in Greenland vary significantly depending on the region and time of year. Coastal areas have milder winters with average temperatures ranging from -10°C to -2°C (14°F to 28°F). Inland areas and higher elevations can be much colder, with average winter temperatures dropping to -20°C (-4°F) or lower.

Precipitation: Precipitation in Greenland is relatively low, particularly in the eastern regions, where it is considered a polar desert. Coastal areas receive more precipitation, mostly in the form of snow. However, the western and southern parts, including the ice-free regions, can experience more rainfall during the summer months.

Seasonal Variation: Greenland has significant seasonal variations in daylight hours. During the summer, the sun remains above the horizon for most of the day, resulting in the phenomenon known as the midnight sun. In contrast, the winter months experience extended periods of darkness with very short daylight hours.

Weather Conditions: Weather conditions in Greenland can change rapidly, and visitors should be prepared for unpredictable weather. Storms, strong winds, and fog are common, especially along the coasts and in the mountainous regions.

When visiting Greenland, it is essential to plan and pack accordingly, taking into account the challenging Arctic climate and the unique natural environment.

Climate and Clothing

Greenland is a distinct and stunning nation with a relatively severe environment, particularly during the winter. It's crucial to dress appropriately and be prepared for the weather conditions in order to ensure that tourists make the most of their stay in Greenland.

It's crucial to keep in mind that Greenland experiences very cold weather while traveling there. With temperatures plunging below zero and frequent snowfall, the winter season may be quite unpleasant. Wearing warm clothes and having appropriate equipment is crucial to being prepared for these situations.

Clothing and gear recommendations for visitors include:

Warm winter jackets: To protect against the weather, they should be windproof and waterproof. Down jackets are a fantastic alternative since they are light and provide superior insulation.

During the colder months in Greenland, thermal underwear is a need. In the worst weather, thermal underwear will keep you warm and dry.

Boots: Warm, waterproof boots are a need for visiting Greenland's breathtaking scenery. For excellent grip on the snow and ice, look for boots with high insulation and a strong sole.

Gloves and caps: Wear warm, waterproof gloves and hats to keep your hands and head warm.

Neck warmers and scarves: They will contribute to your protection against the elements by keeping the wind and cold out..

Weather Conditions and Precipitation

Depending on the season, Greenland experiences dramatic weather and precipitation variations. Often, the hardest weather occurs in the winter, when temperatures regularly dip below zero and snowfall is frequent. Although cooler, the summer months are still fairly chilly and might experience unforeseen weather shifts.

Before heading out into the wilderness, it's crucial to check the weather forecast and be ready for abrupt changes in the weather. Travelers to Greenland should always have a map, compass, and knowledge of the region they are going to, as well as fundamental survival skills such as knowing where to locate shelter and how to build a fire.

It might be a beautiful experience to go to Greenland, but it's vital to be ready for the arid weather and temperature. Visitors may experience the beauty and natural marvels of this exceptional and breathtaking nation with the right apparel and equipment.

Economy

The Greenlandic economy is fundamental to the way of life of the inhabitants of this Arctic country.

The economy of Greenland is largely reliant on its natural resources, including fishing, hunting, and tourism. Since it accounts for more than 90% of Greenland's exports and employs around one-third of the population, the fishing sector is the country's greatest economic contributor. In order to boost the value of its fish exports, the nation has recently made investments in the growth of its infrastructure for export and seafood processing.

Visitors to Greenland come to see its stunning beauty, glaciers, and wildlife, which includes polar bears, whales, and seals. Tourism is a booming sector in Greenland. The tourist industry gives local company owners the chance to launch new enterprises including tour companies, lodgings, and restaurants, resulting in the creation of employment and an increase in local tax revenue.

Another potential development sector for the economy of Greenland is mining. The nation has abundant natural resources, including rare earth minerals, gold, diamonds, and iron ore. The government has been making investments in the growth of the mining industry, which might boost the nation's economy in the long run.

Greenland's economy is nevertheless prone to changes in global commodity prices and the consequences of climate change despite its reliance on these natural resources. The nation is making investments in the growth of alternative energy sources as well as other sectors like agriculture and biotechnology in an effort to diversify its economy and lessen its dependency on a single sector.

Greenland is a distinctive location for tourists and visitors who want to experience its natural beauty and discover its culture. The nation is well-positioned to see economic growth and development in the next few years because of its abundant natural resources and expanding industry.

Language and Communication

Travelers visiting this stunning nation will encounter a dynamic language and communication system that is just as intriguing as the surroundings.

Language

The name of Greenland is Kalaallit Nunaat in Inuit, the official language of the country. The major language of the Greenlandic people is Inuit, a member of the Eskimo-Aleut language family.

This language, which is extensively used in everyday conversation, is a significant part of the nation's culture and legacy.

In Greenland, English is also frequently spoken, particularly among young people and in touristic locations. Being able to speak in English will make it simpler for you to go about the nation and interact with the populace.

Communication

Communication is a key component of the wonderful hospitality that the people of Greenland are recognized for. In Greenland, communication is relaxed and amicable, and using someone's first name is commonplace.

It may be difficult for you to connect with the natives if you don't speak Inuit, which is the primary language spoken in the nation.

Nonetheless, if you speak English, you may get along with the populace rather well, particularly in tourist hotspots.

The predominant language of the deaf people in the nation is Greenlandic Sign Language (GSL), which is also commonly spoken. It is crucial to be aware of this if you are taking a deaf person to Greenland and to make sure they have access to a GSL interpreter.

To sum up, learning the language and modes of communication of Greenland is crucial to having a great time when visiting this beautiful nation.

Common Phrases

Here are some common phrases in English and Inuit that you may find useful while traveling in Greenland:

English:

Hello - Aavaka

How are you? - Ku-na-ma-lu-neq?

Fine, thanks - Qa-neq, ta-qan-nag-put

What is your name? - Tusa-na-qat-si-gut?

My name is ... - Si-na-ma-gat ...

Goodbye - Ta-pag-sor-ma-lu

Yes - I-la-qat-tuk

No - Si-na-tuk

Please - Ta-gu-na

Thank you - Ta-qan-nag-put

Inuit:

Hello - Alluit

How are you? - Ku-na-ma-lu-neq?

Fine, thanks - Qa-neq, ta-qan-nag-put

What is your name? - Tusa-na-qat-si-gut?

My name is ... - Si-na-ma-gat ...

Goodbye - Ta-pag-sor-ma-lu

Yes - I-la-qat-tuk

No - Si-na-tuk

Please - Ta-gu-na

Thank you - Ta-qan-nag-put

Note: Inuit pronunciation may vary slightly among regions, but these phrases should help you communicate effectively with the locals.

Best Time to Visit

Knowing the ideal time to visit Greenland is crucial if you want to make the most of your trip and experience.

Depending on what you want to do while you're there, there is no one optimal time to go to Greenland. The summer months of June, July, and August are the finest times to visit if you want the nicest weather.

You may enjoy all the outdoor activities the nation has to offer, including hiking, kayaking, and whale watching, at this season since it is pleasant outside and the days are long.

The winter months of September to April are the greatest times to go if you're interested in seeing the Northern Lights. These months include bright skies, which makes it simpler to witness the aurora borealis' magnificent show. Keep in mind that these months might have exceptionally severe weather, thus it's essential to take warm clothes and equipment.

The spring months of May and June are the ideal times to go if you want to see animals. The whales are migrating this season to the country's warmer waters, making it simpler to see them.

Additionally, the springtime is a rare chance to see the hundreds of birds that migrate to Greenland to breed and lay their eggs.

Greenland has something special to offer at every season of the year. The country's distinctive landscapes and rich cultural legacy will provide you with lifelong memories, whether you're seeking a summer adventure or a winter getaway.

CHAPTER 2

GETTING THERE

Getting to Greenland

The journey there might be a bit intimidating if this is your first time there or you are planning your vacation. But don't worry, we're here to assist you through the process of getting to this far-off place and make your journey as easy and enjoyable as we can.

Getting to Greenland is a voyage in and of itself, and the first step to taking advantage of all the nation has to offer, whether you decide to fly or take a cruise.

Visas and Permits

Travelers and tourists should become acquainted with the many kinds of visas and permissions required to enter, work or study, or visit isolated locations in Greenland. Visas and permits are a crucial component of trip preparation.

Entry Requirements

A current passport and a visa, if necessary, are requirements for visitors to Greenland. Visa-free entrance to Greenland is available to citizens of the EU, the US, Canada, Australia, and New Zealand for stays of up to 90 days. The Danish Embassy in your home country is where you must apply for a visa if you want to remain for more than 90 days.

Work and Study Visas

A different visa will be necessary for anyone who wants to work or study in Greenland. It is advised that visitors seek expert advice to guide them through the lengthier and more difficult visa procedure for employment and study.

Travelers need to have a job offer or a letter of admission from a university, proof of health insurance, and documentation of their financial support in order to be qualified for a work or study visa.

Travel Permits for Remote Areas

Visitors must get a travel permission from the neighborhood police station in order to go to distant parts of Greenland, such as the northern and eastern regions. Travelers who want to tour these places must get these travel permits, which are necessary for safety and security reasons.

While applying for a travel permit is simple, passengers should be ready to provide specifics about their trip intentions, equipment, and emergency preparations.

Visitors are advised to remain current on the most recent rules since Greenland's visa and permission requirements are subject to change. The process of obtaining a visa or permission may be time-consuming and requires meticulous planning, so travelers should plan ahead and get acquainted with the prerequisite stages.

Flights

Even while getting to Greenland, a distant nation in the Arctic, may require some travel, it is well worth the trouble. The most convenient method to get here is by air, and Greenland is home to a number of international airports that provide service to several locations.

There are many possibilities for flights to Greenland, regardless of where you are traveling from in Europe, North America, or elsewhere.

Airlines that fly to Greenland

Despite its difficult geography, the nation is served by a number of airlines that run frequent flights to and from its main cities.

Here is a list of some of the airlines that fly tourists to Greenland:

Greenland Air: The main airline operating in Greenland is Air Greenland, which serves as the nation's flag carrier. It offers flights to Iceland, many locations in Europe, including Copenhagen, Kangerlussuaq, Nuuk, and Ilulissat, as well as places inside Greenland. Additionally, Air Greenland provides scenic flights to some of Greenland's most stunning natural features, such as glaciers and ice fjords.

SAS: From Copenhagen, SAS (Scandinavian Airlines), a Scandinavian airline, offers flights to Greenland. In addition to weekly flights to other locations in the nation, the airline offers daily service to Nuuk, the capital of Greenland. Given that the airline provides connecting flights from a number of destinations in the area, SAS is a well-liked option for visitors who wish to go to Greenland from Europe or the United States.

Air Iceland Connect: From Reykjavik, Icelandic airline Air Iceland Connect offers flights to Greenland. Flights are offered by the airline to a number of locations in Greenland, such as Kangerlussuaq, Ilulissat, and Narsarsuaq. Visitors seeking for a direct route from Iceland to Greenland might choose Air Iceland Connect.

Polar Umiaq Line Greenlandic ferry company Arctic Umiaq Line offers tourists an unique way to travel. Visitors may enjoy the breathtaking scenery and vibrant villages of

Greenland thanks to the company's passenger and freight ship operations connecting a number of locations there. Visitors who wish to discover Greenland's remote villages and towns can take the Arctic Umiaq Line.

There are a number of airlines that fly to and from Greenland, including the national airline Air Greenland, SAS, Air Iceland Connect, and ferry company Arctic Umiaq Line. It's crucial to verify with the airlines for the most recent information and timetables since flight availability and destinations may change based on the season and weather.

Arrivals and Departures

You must be aware of specific details and prerequisites while entering and leaving Greenland as they may have an impact on your travel arrangements.

Here are some important details to bear in mind:

Getting to the airport: Travelers must show a current passport or ID card at the Greenland airport upon arrival. It can also be necessary to get a visa, depending on your place of origin. For the most recent information on visa requirements, it's crucial to contact the local embassy or consulate. Travelers will also need to fill out a customs declaration form and their bags can be checked when they arrive.

Getting on a plane: Depending on the airline and the destination, different flights to and from Greenland have different check-in times. It's critical to check with your airline for the most up-to-date information and to leave plenty of time before your departure to go to the airport. The majority of airlines demand that passengers check in 60 to 90 minutes before departure.

Baggage restrictions: Baggage restrictions differ according to the airline and level of travel. It's crucial to confirm the most recent details on luggage prices and allowances with your airline. Most airlines let travelers check one bag for free and bring one piece of carry-on luggage. However, there can be charges for oversize or extra luggage.

Taxes imposed on tourists leaving the nation by the local government are known as departure taxes. Departure taxes are often included in the cost of a flight to Greenland. The most recent information on departure taxes should be confirmed with your airline or travel agency.

Customs and security: Travelers must pass through security and customs before leaving Greenland. In most cases, this entails going through a metal detector and having your luggage X-rayed. If security officers believe a passenger is carrying restricted or forbidden materials, they may additionally ask the traveler to submit to a pat-down search.

You must be ready and knowledgeable about the regulations for traveling to and from Greenland, such as airline check-in hours, baggage restrictions, departure charges, and security and customs processes. You may make sure that your arrival and departure from Greenland go smoothly and without worry by adhering to these recommendations and staying up to date with the most recent information.

Flight Availability and Schedules

Flight availability and schedules to and from Greenland might change based on the season and the state of the weather. Here are some crucial details to bear in mind as you prepare for your trip:

Seasonality: Seasonal variations may have an impact on travel itineraries to and from Greenland, with more flights being offered in the warmer summer months. Due to bad weather, flight schedules may be shortened or canceled throughout the winter.

You need to confirm the most recent flight schedules and availability with your airline.

Flight frequency: Depending on the airline and the destination, flights to and from Greenland vary in frequency. Greenland may only have a few flights per week to certain locations, while daily flights may be available to others. It's critical to confirm the most recent flight schedules and availability with your airline.

Connection flights: You may need to take a connecting flight if you're traveling to Greenland from a location outside of Europe or North America. Usually, connecting flights are offered via Reykjavik or Copenhagen (Denmark) (Iceland). The airline and the destination will determine the availability and timing of connecting flights.

Flight time: Depending on the airline and route, the time it takes to fly from major cities to Greenland might vary. For instance, direct flights from Copenhagen to Nuuk usually last for around two hours. The normal flight time from Reykjavik to a Greenland location is one to two hours.

Booking in advance: Especially during the busiest travel season, booking your flight to or from Greenland in advance is advised. By doing this, you may guarantee a seat on the aircraft of your choice and avoid disappointment brought on by overbooking.

The availability and timing of flights to and from Greenland might change based on the season, the weather, and the airline. You can make sure you have a pleasant and stress-free trip by contacting your airline to find out the most recent flight schedules and options.

Ferries

Ferries are a popular mode of transportation for tourists entering the nation since they provide a more leisurely and picturesque route to their desired locations. Everything you need to know about taking ferries to Greenland will be covered here, including the various ferry routes, the kinds of boats that are available, what to anticipate on board, and what to bring for your trip.

Routes and Options

Greenland is connected to neighboring nations by a number of ferry routes, notably Iceland and Denmark. The majority of tourists to the nation will start their journeys on the main route, which runs between Iceland and the west coast of Greenland.

There are two primary ferry companies operating this route, Smyril Line and Arctic Umiaq Line. Regular sailings between Seydisfjordur in Iceland and Qaqortoq in Greenland are provided by both companies, with stops at the Faroe Islands and other locations en route.

The MV Norröna is a contemporary ferry operated by Smyril Line that has cozy accommodations, a restaurant, and a variety of on-board amenities including a theater, a kids' play area, and a shopping arcade.

The MV Sara, operated by Arctic Umiaq Line, is a smaller ferry with fewer facilities but still provides comfortable seats, a restaurant, and several chances to take in the spectacular scenery.

What to Expect on Board

No matter which ferry company you go on, you can anticipate a pleasant and laid-back trip with lots of opportunity to take in the landscape and get to know your fellow travelers. The majority of ferries have inviting sitting spaces, a restaurant selling a variety of delectable meals, and a range of recreational alternatives, including live music, movies, and games.

You may choose from a variety of cabins for lodging, including individual rooms, family rooms, and shared bunk rooms. Every cabin comes with a cozy bed, a private bathroom, and plenty of storage for your possessions.

What to Pack for Your Journey

Be sure to pack appropriately for the varied weather and sea conditions before boarding the ship for Greenland. The following are some things you must bring with you:

Pack lots of warm gear, including a coat, hat, gloves, and heavy boots, since Greenland can be quite cold, particularly when going by boat.

Bringing waterproof clothes, such as a raincoat or poncho, can help you stay protected from the elements in Greenland, where the weather is prone to being erratic.

Medicine for motion sickness: If you often get seasick, pack some medication to assist you avoid any pain while traveling.

Bring some books, games, or other forms of entertainment to keep oneself engaged while on board to help pass the time.

Camera: Make sure to pack a camera so you can document the beautiful surroundings and memories of your trip.

For travelers seeking a laid-back and fun vacation, ferries to Greenland provide a distinctive and picturesque method to reach the nation. Whether you decide to travel with Smyril Line or Arctic Umiaq Line, you can count on an enjoyable trip with lots of chances to take in the surroundings and get to know your fellow passengers.

Operators and Routes

Smyril Line and Arctic Umiaq Line are the two primary ferry companies that provide services to Greenland.

The MV Norröna is operated by Smyril Line, and it travels through the Faroe Islands, Torshavn, and other locations from Seydisfjordur, Iceland to Qaqortoq, Greenland. Tourists who wish to see the country's breathtaking beauty and animals often choose this route.

The MV Sara is run by Arctic Umiaq Line, and it travels from Reykjavik, Iceland, to Nuuk, the capital of Greenland. Compared to the Smyril Line line, this one is more rudimentary, yet it still provides a relaxing and delightful experience.

Schedules and Pricing

Ferries to Greenland have different timetables and costs depending on the company and the route.

Regular sailings between Seydisfjordur, Iceland and Qaqortoq, Greenland, are provided by Smyril Line; one-way tickets start at around $200. The firm provides a variety of cabin alternatives, with costs varied according to the cabin type you choose. These options include private rooms, family rooms, and shared bunk rooms.

A one-way ticket on Arctic Umiaq Line's regular service between Reykjavik, Iceland, and Nuuk, Greenland, costs around $150. There are just a few cabins available from the firm, and they may be rented in advance.

It is crucial to remember that the cost of ferries to Greenland may change depending on the season, with peak season costs often being higher than off-season costs. It is advised to purchase your boat tickets well in advance in order to receive the greatest value.

With several companies and routes available, ferries to Greenland provide a distinctive and picturesque means of travel to the nation. Prices for one-way tickets start at around $150, and both Smyril Line and Arctic Umiaq Line will provide you with a relaxing and enjoyable trip.

Cruises

A cruise to Greenland is an exciting and daring approach to discover the biggest island in the world. Greenland is a distinctive, far-flung location in the North Atlantic that is both wild and stunning, and it offers a plethora of natural beauties, wildlife, and cultural experiences.

The beautiful scenery and unique ecosystems of Greenland, which include glaciers, fjords, mountains, and tundra, are well known. In addition to marveling at the towering glaciers and icebergs, visitors can get up close and personal with whales, seals, and other marine life by taking a picturesque boat tour or kayaking journey through the glaciers and ice-capped fjords.

With a fusion of Inuit and Scandinavian elements, Greenland has a vibrant and unique culture. The traditional Inuit way of life, including hunting, fishing, craftsmanship, and storytelling, is available for tourists to learn about. They may also visit museums and cultural institutions that highlight Greenland's history and culture, as well as the tiny towns and villages along the shore.

A variety of excursions and activities are available on the Greenland trip, such as dog sledding, snowmobiling, fishing, and whale viewing. There are several outdoor pursuits available for thrill-seekers, including ice-caving, glacier hiking, and kayaking.

Visit the Ilulissat Icefjord, a UNESCO World Heritage site and one of the most well-known ice fjords in the world, for a really exceptional experience. Massive glaciers that calve into the water in this fjord produce jaw-dropping ice creations that are simply amazing.

A fantastic chance to observe the Northern Lights, one of nature's most amazing displays, is provided by the voyage to Greenland. From late September to early April, when the long evenings and bright sky provide for ideal viewing conditions, is the greatest time to watch the northern lights.

The cruise ships that go to Greenland provide luxurious staterooms, mouth watering dining selections, and a variety of entertainment and recreational alternatives. Visitors may take part in sports and activities, see live performances and music, relax in the spa, or work out in the gym.

A voyage to Greenland is a once-in-a-lifetime opportunity that combines the natural beauty, cultural diversity, and adventure in a unique way. A cruise to Greenland is certain to be a once-in-a-lifetime experience, regardless of whether you are an adventurous traveler, a nature lover, or a culture aficionado.

Popular Cruise Lines Visiting Greenland:

- Hurtigruten

- Princess Cruises

- Royal Caribbean International

- Silversea Cruises

- Seabourn

Ports of Call:

- Nuuk, the capital city of Greenland

- Sisimiut, a historic town in western Greenland

- Ilulissat, known for its UNESCO World Heritage Site,

- Qaqortoq, a charming town in southern Greenland with stunning landscapes and cultural attractions

Getting Around

Being sparsely inhabited and with a dearth of public transit, Greenland may be difficult to navigate. This comprehensive handbook will help you navigate Greenland for the first time.

Travel by Air: The easiest and quickest method to go about in Greenland is via air. There are several airports in the nation, including those at Nuuk, Sisimiut, Ilulissat, and Kangerlussuaq. You may travel to the majority of the nation from these airports thanks to Air Greenland's frequent service. The cost of tickets will be considerable, too, since Greenland has costly air travel.

Boat and Ferry: During the summer, boats and ferries are an excellent method to travel around Greenland's coast. There are boats that sail between villages on the east coast of Greenland, and you may take a ferry from Nuuk to Ilulissat and other coastal towns. However, ferries and boats are not always dependable, and the weather might cause schedule changes.

Bus: Greenland has a meager public transportation system, however places like Nuuk and Sisimiut do have buses. These buses follow a regular schedule and provide a comfortable and reasonably priced means of transportation.

Bus timetables may be constrained, and certain isolated areas might not be accessible by bus.

Taxi: Taxis are a practical method to move about and are accessible in most cities in Greenland. Be aware that Greenland's taxis are more costly than those in other nations, so plan accordingly.

Renting a vehicle: If you want to really see Greenland, renting a car is a terrific way to travel about. You may hire a vehicle in Nuuk, Kangerlussuaq, and other significant cities thanks to the many automobile rental agencies in the nation. However, be ready to pay expensive rental rates, and remember that driving in Greenland may be difficult, particularly in the winter.

Although traveling in Greenland might be difficult, it can still be pleasurable with the correct preparation. Make sure to do your homework to find the ideal route for your vacation.

CHAPTER 3

ACCOMMODATION

Accommodation in Greenland

Visitors have a variety of lodging alternatives in Greenland, a secluded and beautiful location. Whether you're looking for comfort, adventure, or a combination of both, there are accommodations for everyone, from little bed & breakfasts to opulent hotels.

In Greenland, lodging options vary from simple cabins in the countryside to chic, contemporary hotels in the towns. The stunning views of the mountains, fjords, and glaciers from many of the houses provide for a genuinely immersive experience.

Types of Accommodation

Greenland is a far-flung, inhospitable location with a variety of lodging alternatives to meet visitors' demands. Everyone may find something to enjoy in this unusual and intriguing nation, which offers everything from modest bed & breakfasts to opulent hotels.

You can discover the ideal lodging in Greenland, whether you're seeking for a base from which to explore the breathtaking landscapes or a plush, comfortable spot to unwind and recharge.

Here, we'll examine the many lodging options in Greenland, ranging from classic Inuit lodges to cutting-edge hotels and everything in between.

Therefore, in this lovely and secluded location, you are sure to discover the ideal spot to stay, whether you are seeking for an affordable choice or a deluxe getaway.

Hotels

Hotels in Greenland come at a variety of price points, from inexpensive to opulent. In addition to more modest hotels and guesthouses in nearby towns and villages, the capital city of Nuuk has a number of contemporary, luxurious hotels. With features like en-suite bathrooms, Wi-Fi, and TVs, these hotels provide guests with cozy, spotless accommodations.

For those looking for a convenient and pleasant base from which to explore Greenland, several hotels also provide eating choices, exercise centers, and other amenities.

There are some upscale hotels in Greenland that provide first-rate amenities and services, such as spas, restaurants, and stunning views of the surrounding landscapes, for those seeking a more opulent stay. These lodgings are suitable for honeymoons and other romantic holidays for individuals who wish to unwind and indulge in a little pampering.

Here are some hotel ideas for visitors to Greenland:

Hotel Arctic, Ilulissat: This hotel is located in Ilulissat, which is known for its UNESCO World Heritage site, the Ilulissat Icefjord. The hotel offers stunning views of the icefjord and the surrounding landscapes. It also has a restaurant that serves local and international cuisine.

Hotel Hans Egede, Nuuk: This hotel is located in the capital city of Greenland, Nuuk. It offers comfortable rooms, a restaurant serving local and international cuisine, and a bar. It's a great place to stay if you want to explore the city and its attractions.

Hotel Kulusuk, Kulusuk: This hotel is located on the island of Kulusuk, which is known for its breathtaking landscapes and traditional Inuit culture. The hotel offers cozy rooms, a restaurant serving local cuisine, and tours of the surrounding area.

Hotel Sisimiut, Sisimiut: This hotel is located in the town of Sisimiut, which is known for its outdoor activities like hiking, skiing, and dog-sledding. The hotel offers comfortable rooms, a restaurant serving local cuisine, and easy access to the town's attractions.

Hotel Nordbo, Ilulissat: This hotel is located in Ilulissat and offers modern and spacious apartments with stunning views of the Ilulissat Icefjord. It's a great place to stay if you want more space and privacy during your visit to Greenland.

Hotels are a great option for many types of tourists, from lone explorers to families, since they provide a variety of amenities and services.

Hostels

Travelers may find affordable lodging alternatives in Greenland in hostels. These hostels often provide dorm-style lodging with communal spaces and shared bedrooms.

They are a fantastic choice for anyone looking to see Greenland on a tight budget, including backpackers, students, and those on a tight budget.

The majority of hostels in Greenland are well-equipped, with spotless amenities including communal kitchens, common areas, and restrooms. They provide a social setting where one may meet other tourists and exchange tales of their travels.

Hostels in Greenland provide a convenient and budget-friendly way to see this breathtaking location, whether you're traveling alone, with friends, or with your family. Hostels are a great option for tourists on a tight budget who want to have a distinctive and memorable experience in Greenland since they place a strong emphasis on price, comfort, and a social environment.

Here are some hostel ideas for visitors to Greenland:

The Arctic Hostel: Located in the town of Ilulissat, this hostel offers breathtaking views of the Ilulissat Icefjord, which is a UNESCO World Heritage Site. The hostel provides private rooms and shared dormitories, and guests can enjoy the beautiful scenery from the outdoor terrace or relax in the cozy common room.

Qaqortoq Hostel: Situated in the charming town of Qaqortoq, this hostel is a perfect base for exploring the southern part of Greenland. The hostel provides private rooms and shared dormitories, and guests can enjoy the communal kitchen and lounge area.

Nuuk Hostel: Located in the capital city of Nuuk, this hostel is a great option for travelers who want to explore the city's museums, galleries, and restaurants. The hostel provides private rooms and shared dormitories, and guests can enjoy the outdoor terrace and common room.

Kangerlussuaq Hostel: This hostel is located in the small town of Kangerlussuaq, which is a popular starting point for exploring the Greenland Ice Sheet. The hostel provides private rooms and shared dormitories, and guests can enjoy the communal kitchen and lounge area.

Sisimiut Hostel: Situated in the picturesque town of Sisimiut, this hostel is a perfect base for exploring the surrounding mountains and fjords. The hostel provides private rooms and shared dormitories, and guests can enjoy the communal kitchen and lounge area.

Campsites

Greenland's campgrounds provide an unique and affordable opportunity to take in the breathtaking scenery and unspoiled beauty of this far-off nation. Camping in Greenland is a well-liked alternative for tourists who wish to get close to nature and enjoy the great outdoors because of the variety of accommodations available, from basic tent sites to RV parks.

Camping in Greenland is an inexpensive and memorable experience, whether you're going alone, with friends, or with your family. Campsites are a great option for those who wish to enjoy the best of Greenland on a budget since they place a strong emphasis on affordability, a connection to nature, and a range of activities and excursions.

Camping in Greenland is a memorable experience that is likely to be enjoyed for years to come because of the breathtaking scenery, the abundance of activities and excursions, and the emphasis on cost.

Recommended Accommodations in Greenland

There are many different lodging alternatives in Greenland, ranging from inexpensive hostels to opulent hotels and everything in between. The following hotels in Greenland are suggested for various categories of visitors:

Hotel Arctic - Situated in Ilulissat, Hotel Arctic is a five-star establishment with a restaurant, bar, spa, and breathtaking views of the area.

Hotel Hans Egede is a stylish, up-to-date hotel with welcoming rooms, a restaurant, and a bar that is located in the capital city of Nuuk.

Guesthouse Panorama is a budget-friendly inn with clean, comfortable rooms, a common kitchen, and access to outdoor areas that is situated in Sisimiut.

The rural East Greenland village of Kulusuk is home to this charming and pleasant hotel. It provides pleasant accommodations and wonderful views of the surroundings.

Ilulissat Campsite - Located in Ilulissat, this well-liked campground provides beautiful views and convenient access to outdoor activities and excursions.

The charming and comfortable Himmelbjerget Cottage is close to Ilulissat and provides access to outdoor activities as well as breathtaking views of the surrounding area.

The capital city of Nuuk is home to the affordable Nuuk Youth Hostel, which provides a welcoming environment and convenient amenities for tourists on a tight budget.

These are only a handful of the suggested lodgings in Greenland, which provide a variety of possibilities for visitors of different financial abilities and tastes. Greenland has plenty to offer everyone, whether you're seeking a lavish getaway or a frugal excursion.

CHAPTER 4

ACTIVITIES AND ATTRACTIONS

Outdoor Activities

Greenland is a place of unspoiled natural beauty, untamed terrain, and a wealth of species. Greenland has a wide range of thrilling outdoor activities, including kayaking, dog sledding, and hiking. Whether you enjoy the outdoors or are an adrenaline addict, Greenland offers an amazing outdoor experience.

Greenland provides a distinctive and alluring setting for outdoor activities with its magnificent glaciers, high mountains, and pristine lakes. There are a variety of outdoor activities available in Greenland, from the fjords and glaciers on the east coast to the untamed tundra in the west.

Snowmobiling and Dog Sledding

In Greenland, two of the most popular winter sports are snowmobiling and dog sledding. These pursuits provide a unique chance to take in this vast and distant nation's breathtaking, untainted nature and stunning vistas.

Snowmobiling is a fascinating activity that enables you to discover Greenland's lonely and stunning landscape. Greenland is the ideal location for a snowmobile excursion because of its vast, snow-covered landscape and undulating hills.

The glaciers, mountains, and frozen fjords may all be seen in amazing detail on snowmobiling trips, which can last anything from a few hours to several days. Snowmobiles are simple to use, making them an excellent choice for both novice and seasoned riders.

Another well-liked winter sport in Greenland is dog sledding, which offers a very genuine glimpse into the native culture of the region. Teams of sled dogs that have been taught to pull sleds through snow-covered terrain often participate in dog sledding excursions.

Strong and tenacious, these dogs have a long history of being employed as sled dogs in the Arctic areas. The experience of sledding through the snow-covered wilderness while being surrounded by stunning glaciers and mountains is certainly one-of-a-kind and memorable.

Both snowmobile and dog sledding are well-liked sports for both residents and tourists, and they both provide a unique way to see the landscape and culture of Greenland. Snowmobiling and dog sledding are guaranteed to be a remarkable experience, whether you're an experienced winter explorer or simply searching for a new and exciting way to enjoy the beauty of Greenland.

Kayaking and Rafting

In Greenland, rafting and kayaking are two of the most popular water sports. Kayaking and rafting are great ways to experience the nation's breathtaking coastal scenery throughout the summer, when the rivers and fjords are free of ice.

Experience the splendor of Greenland's fjords, inlets, and glaciers by kayaking. Kayaking in Greenland offers a private and tranquil opportunity to encounter the outdoors because of its clear seas.

Greenland offers a variety of kayaking experiences, making it suited for both novice and expert paddlers, from serene lakes to swift-moving whitewater.

Another well-liked water sport in Greenland is rafting, which provides a more adventurous and exhilarating experience.

In Greenland, rafting excursions take you through the nation's swift-moving rivers while being surrounded by soaring mountains, glaciers, and waterfalls. Rafting in Greenland is certain to be an amazing experience, regardless of whether you are an expert rafter or just searching for an exhilarating new adventure.

Both kayaking and rafting provide a unique approach to take in Greenland's beauty and nature. These activities are guaranteed to provide visitors to this beautiful nation an amazing experience, whether they desire a quiet and private trip on the water or one that is more exciting and daring.

Ice-caving and Glacier Trekking

Ice-caving and glacier hiking are two well-liked wintertime pursuits in Greenland that provide an unique and breath-taking perspective of the nation's magnificent ice formations.

Visitors may explore the complex and unearthly beauty of Greenland's glaciers from inside by engaging in the unusual practice of ice-caving. Visitors may see the breathtaking beauty of ice formations, such as blue ice caves and crystal-clear ice sculptures, by taking ice-caving trips that lead them deep into glaciers. For those who wish to see the magnificence of Greenland's glaciers up close and personal, this activity is amazing.

Another well-liked winter activity is glacier hiking, which lets tourists explore the Greenland glaciers on foot. Visitors are taken on glacier hiking trips where they may see the breathtaking grandeur of these old ice formations and gain a feel of the glaciers' size.

Hiking on the glaciers is a one-of-a-kind and spectacular adventure that provides breathtaking views of the surrounding area, including imposing peaks and snow-covered valleys.

The majesty of Greenland's glaciers may be appreciated in an unique and magnificent manner via both ice-caving and glacier hiking. These pursuits are well-liked by both residents and tourists, and they are appropriate for people of all ages and fitness levels.

Ice-caving and glacier trekking in Greenland are guaranteed to provide a genuinely remarkable experience, whether you're an experienced adventurer or simply searching for a new and thrilling adventure.

Cultural Attractions

The severe climate and rocky terrain of Greenland have sculpted the nation's rich cultural legacy, giving it a distinct and interesting identity. Greenland is a culturally rich region that is just waiting to be discovered, with everything from the vibrant wooden dwellings of the Inuit inhabitants to the breathtaking fjords and glaciers that dominate the landscapes.

The rich history and traditions of Greenland are on display in a variety of cultural attractions available to tourists, including museums, cultural institutions, and historical sites. There is something to discover and admire around every corner, from the renowned Inuit art and handmade objects to the vibrant houses and communities that dot the shoreline.

There is no lack of cultural things to discover, whether your interests lie in discovering the history of the Inuit people, discovering the thriving local arts and crafts sector, or just taking in Greenland's breathtaking natural beauty.

Museums and Galleries

Greenland's museums and galleries provide a unique insight into the rich history, culture, and customs of this far-flung yet compelling nation. Visitors to Greenland will find an abundance of cultural treasures waiting to be found, including the distinctive Inuit art and handmade items as well as the colorful dwellings and communities that dot the coastline.

Visitors may discover the history and culture of the Inuit people, from their earliest nomadic origins to their contemporary villages, at the National Museum of Greenland in Nuuk. The museum displays a vast assortment of objects and works of history, including carved ivory statues, artisanal equipment and clothes, and traditional musical instruments.

The Katuaq Cultural Center in Nuuk is a must-see for art enthusiasts as it features the creations of regional performers and artists and hosts a variety of cultural events and exhibits. Visitors may get a taste of Greenland's thriving cultural life here, which includes everything from modern art and music to traditional dance and storytelling.

Visitors may also find local galleries and exhibits in smaller towns and villages that feature the creations of regional artists and artisans, providing a unique and genuine view into Greenland's cultural life. These galleries and shows are a veritable gold mine of artistic inspiration, with colorful paintings and sculptures as well as handmade jewelry and ceramics.

Hence, museums and galleries offer a distinctive and remarkable approach to understand the culture of this far-off and alluring nation, whether you are a history enthusiast, an art enthusiast, or just interested in learning about the rich and intriguing legacy of Greenland.

Historical Sites and Monuments

Visitors to the nation will discover a multitude of historical sites and monuments to see since Greenland has a long and intriguing history. Greenland has a rich tapestry of history that is just waiting to be found, ranging from prehistoric Inuit dwellings and trade sites to colonial structures and contemporary monuments.

One of the most well-known historical sites in Greenland is the Ilulissat Icefjord, a UNESCO World Heritage Site that exhibits the spectacular majesty of the country's glaciers and fjords. Tourists may go on a boat excursion to see the breathtaking scenery and discover the region's geological past.

In southern Greenland, close to Narsarsuaq, lies the remains of the Hvals Church, another important historical site. This ancient church, which was built in the 17th century, is a reminder of Greenland's first days as a colony.

Visitors may tour the historic Hans Egede monument in the capital city of Nuuk, which honors the arrival of the first Danish missionaries in Greenland in the early eighteenth century. The monument is located in front of the well-known St. Anna's Church, one of the oldest in the nation and a reminder of the rich religious tradition of the nation.

The Sisimiut Museum, which chronicles the history of the Inuit people and the neighborhood, and the Viking ruins at the Herjolfsnes settlement, which provide a look into early Norse occupation of Greenland, are two more noteworthy historical sites in Greenland.

There are plenty of historical sites and monuments to uncover in this isolated and alluring nation, whether you are a history buff, an archaeology enthusiast, or just interested in learning about the rich and interesting legacy of Greenland.

Wildlife in Greenland

Greenland is a distinctive and lovely location that provides a wide variety of animal encounters. Greenland is a nature lover's heaven, from the beautiful whales that ply its seas to the majestic polar bears who make the island home.

Whale watching is one of the most popular activities in Greenland, and tourists from all over the world go here to see these amazing animals in their natural environment. Humpback, minke, and sperm whales are just a few of the many whale species that inhabit the waters of Greenland. These whales are renowned for their playful nature and their enormous size, which makes them awe-inspiring to see.

With so many different bird species living on the island, birdwatching is another well-liked pastime in Greenland. Birdwatchers will have enough to do, from the vivid and brilliant Arctic terns to the stately and royal eagles. The island's many fjords and lakes serve as ideal homes for waterfowl, giving for some fantastic possibilities for bird watching.

Sightings of polar bears are another well-liked attraction for tourists in Greenland. These majestic animals, whose beauty and strength are simply breathtaking, wander the island's ice-covered landscapes.

In the spring and summer, when they are more likely to walk onto ice floes in search of food, is the greatest time to watch polar bears.

Lastly, the seas around Greenland are home to several seal and walrus populations, offering a unique and intriguing chance to witness these majestic animals in their native environment.

The walruses and seals are renowned for their lively and inquisitive demeanor, and they are often seen in big groups. Visitors visiting Greenland are likely to have a once-in-a-lifetime experience when swimming or sunbathing at these colonies.

Very diverse animal encounters may be had in Greenland, from seeing whales and birds to seeing polar bears, seal, and walrus populations.

Greenland is a place not to be missed, whether you are an experienced wildlife enthusiast or are just hoping to enjoy the grandeur and majesty of the natural environment.

Must Visit Destinations

You will be in awe of the captivating natural beauty known as Ilulissat Icefjord in Greenland. Some of the most stunning and breathtaking glaciers in the whole world may be seen in this fjord, which is a UNESCO World Heritage site.

The size of the glaciers in Ilulissat Icefjord is one of its most amazing features. At a pace of almost 20 meters per day, the Sermeq Kujalleq glacier is the one that is moving the quickest in the whole globe.

Almost 10% of the ice that flows into the ocean from Greenland is produced by this one glacier alone. The glacier, which rises up to 200 meters above sea level, is encircled by stunning scenery and high mountains that provide breath-taking vistas.

Whales, seals, birds, and other animals of all kinds may be found at Ilulissat Icefjord. Visitors may get up and personal with the gorgeous animals as they move across the fjord. The fjord is a well-liked location for ice trekking and kayaking, offering an exciting trip for those seeking a thrill.

Ilulissat Icefjord has a fascinating cultural heritage in addition to its natural beauty. The Inuit, who have lived in the area for a long time, have a deep connection to the land and its glaciers. During guided tours and cultural presentations, visitors may learn about Inuit culture and way of life.

Anybody wishing for an amazing journey should visit Ilulissat Icefjord, an unique and spectacular natural phenomenon. Everyone visiting Greenland should go there because of its glaciers, wildlife, and extensive cultural past.

Diverso Bay

Beautiful Disko Bay may be found on Greenland's western shore. This harbor is home to several rare animal species and is bordered by imposing mountains and glaciers.

Disko Bay is renowned for its beautiful scenery and amazing beauty. Magnificent glaciers, imposing mountains, and stunning fjords surround the bay, providing sweeping vistas of the surrounding landscape. Since it is also home to a wide variety of species, including whales, seals, and birds, this bay is a well-known area for wildlife watching.

Disko Bay has a rich cultural past in addition to its natural beauty. The Inuit, who have lived in the area for a long time, have a close relationship with the land and its fauna. During guided tours and cultural presentations, visitors may learn about Inuit culture and way of life.

Kayaking, ice trekking, and fishing are among the outdoor activities and adventure sports that are popular in Disko Bay. Visitors may discover Disko Bay's breathtaking sceneries while having an amazing time with these activities.

Kangerlussuaq

Western Greenland's Kangerlussuaq is a little town with a fascinating history that is often disregarded by tourists. It serves as a starting point for exploring Greenland's immense wilderness, which is home to stunning scenery and exciting activities.

The settlement of Kangerlussuaq is located on the banks of the vast Kangerlussuaq Fjord, and its name, which translates to "great fjord" in the Inuit language, is appropriate. The fjord is a significant center for trade and transportation since it provides a natural harbor for boats and ships.

Since the American military built a base there during World War II to aid the Allies in Europe, Kangerlussuaq has had a colorful history. After the war, the facility continued to be utilized as a stopover for transatlantic flights up until the 1990s.

The former runway is now a well-traveled route for bicycling and hiking, with breathtaking vistas of the forest beyond.

The Arctic Tundra is one of Kangerlussuaq's most distinctive and stunning characteristics. A remarkable variety of plants and animals may be found in the tundra, a wide, treeless plain that extends as far as the eye can see. Explore the tundra on foot or on horseback to see Arctic foxes, reindeer, musk oxen, and a variety of bird species.

Kangerlussuaq has a never-ending supply of exciting chances for outdoor lovers. A few of the activities include dog sledding, fishing, hiking, and kayaking. In addition, the town is a well-liked winter sports destination, with miles of cross-country skiing and snowmobile routes crisscrossing the picturesque scenery.

It is difficult to find a place that combines history, wilderness, and adventure as Kangerlussuaq does.

Nuuk

The dynamic and culturally diverse capital of Greenland serves as a showcase for the finest that the nation has to offer. Nuuk, the capital of Greenland and its biggest city, is a center for politics, business, and culture. It is situated on the Davis Strait's coastlines.

The National Museum of Greenland, which gives tourists a thorough look at the nation's history from the Inuit people to the advent of the Europeans, is one of Nuuk's most prominent attractions.

The museum also has an amazing collection of antiquities and cultural relics, including sculptures, hunting equipment, and traditional costumes.

The Katuaq Cultural Centre, a beautiful structure that serves as a center for the arts in Greenland, is another must-see location in Nuuk. The center serves as a focal point for the city's creative community and offers performances, exhibits, and cultural events.

Nuuk has a ton of exciting options for outdoor lovers. Although the shore is a well-liked location for kayaking and fishing, the adjacent mountains provide fantastic hiking and skiing options. Fjords and bays that provide beautiful vistas, possibilities for boat cruises, and whale viewing are available all around the city.

The food scene in Nuuk is likewise thriving and diversified, with a variety of eateries serving everything from authentic Inuit fare to foreign cuisine. Visitors may try regional delicacies including Arctic char and reindeer meat as well as savor freshly caught fish from the area's waterways.

It is possible to get insight into Greenland's rich history and culture by visiting Nuuk, a distinctive and intriguing location. Nuuk is a must-visit location for every Greenland tourist, whether they want to take in the colorful atmosphere, explore the city's museums and cultural institutions, or go out into nature for some adventure.

Sisimiut

Sisimiut, also known as Holsteinsborg, is the second-largest town in Greenland and is a seaside community in the country's central-west region. With around 6,000 residents, it is a thriving community that provides a distinctive fusion of contemporary conveniences and traditional Inuit culture.

There are many options for tourists visiting Sisimiut to take advantage of the breathtaking natural beauty of the region, including the glaciers, fjords, and mountains close by. The Sisimiut Adventure Park, which provides a variety of outdoor activities including kayaking, fishing, and hiking, is one of the most well-liked attractions in the region.

The Sisimiut Museum, which highlights the area's rich cultural legacy and offers a thorough look at the history and traditions of the Inuit people, is another must-see destination. The museum offers tourists a unique view into the life of the people of Sisimiut and has an extraordinary collection of traditional Inuit art and artifacts.

There are many options for people who want to fully immerse themselves in the culture to do so. Visitors may take in traditional Inuit dance performances, eat local food at one of the numerous eateries, or shop for handcrafted goods and souvenirs at the neighborhood market.

From affordable hostels and guesthouses to opulent hotels and resorts, Sisimiut provides a variety of lodging alternatives to suit all interests and budgets. Also, the town boasts a lively nightlife that offers guests a wide range of pubs, nightclubs, and live music venues.

Overall, Sisimiut is a lively and friendly town that gives tourists the chance to take in the rich cultural legacy of the area while also taking use of contemporary conveniences and outdoor pursuits. Sisimiut offers activities for everyone, whether you want to discover the region's natural beauty, learn about the Inuit people's history and traditions, or just unwind and take in the atmosphere.

Qaqortoq

The picturesque seaside community of Qaqortoq, sometimes called Julianehb, is situated in the southern part of Greenland. It is the biggest community on the southern shore and the fourth-largest town in the nation, giving it the perfect place for tourists to explore Greenland's distinctive beauty and culture.

Several of the town's structures are from the 18th and 19th centuries, and they are well-known for their historical architecture. This contains the yellow-painted Hans Egede House, the oldest still-existing structure in Greenland, which was constructed in 1734. The town is also home to a number of other historic residences and structures, in addition to a museum devoted to local history.

The Qaqortoq Stone and Bronze Age Centre, one of the city's most well-liked tourist destinations, provides tourists with an insight into the area's prehistoric history. The Saqqaq, Dorset, and Thule cultures, as well as other early Greenlandic indigenous cultures, are discussed here, and visitors may examine artifacts from each of these cultures.

Outdoor lovers will find Qaqortoq to be surrounded by outstanding natural scenery, including the nearby fjords and mountains. The surrounding area may be explored on foot, by boat, or even on horseback while admiring the spectacular vistas.

The town is also a center for arts and crafts, with many regional artisans selling their goods in the various stores and studios spread out around the community. Everything from customary Greenlandic attire and accessories to handcrafted jewelry, pottery, and wooden carvings is available to tourists.

Dining choices in Qaqortoq vary from informal cafés and bistros to fine dining establishments and traditional Greenlandic pubs. The local cuisine, which includes delicacies like reindeer stew, halibut, and customary breads made from fermented seaweed, is available for sampling by tourists.

For those who want to immerse themselves in Greenland's rich culture, history, and natural beauty, Qaqortoq is a must-visit location. Whether you like history, the outdoors, or are just searching for a different and interesting experience,

Aasiaat

A tiny settlement in Greenland's west also goes by the name of Egedesminde. The town, which is the fifth biggest in the nation, is renowned for its picturesque surroundings, lively cultural scene, and extensive history.

The village is a fantastic area to go hiking, fishing, and boating since it is surrounded by stunning fjords and mountains. In order to see animals and see the surrounding natural beauty, visitors may also enjoy a picturesque boat cruise around the adjacent islands.

With several museums and cultural establishments that highlight the history and customs of the area, Aasiaat is also endowed with a rich cultural legacy. The most prominent of them is the Aasiaat Museum, which has a variety of relics and displays that depict the town's history, from its earliest years as a fishing hamlet to its present-day position as a bustling municipality.

Also, the community is home to a thriving arts and crafts sector where regional artisans create a broad variety of handcrafted goods including jewelry, pottery, and traditional clothes. Also, tourists may participate in regional cultural events like the yearly Aasiaat Culture Festival, which offers performances, music, and regional cuisine.

Aasiaat has a variety of eating establishments, from laid-back cafés and bistros to more sophisticated eateries that serve traditional Greenlandic food. Local fare such as reindeer stew, shellfish chowder, and customary breads made from fermented seaweed are available for visitors to enjoy.

In summary, Aasiaat is a distinct and endearing town that provides tourists with a look into the rich culture and stunning natural beauty of Greenland. Aasiaat is unquestionably a visit whether you're a history buff, an outdoor enthusiast, or just searching for a distinctive cultural experience.

Qasigiannguit

On the west coast of Greenland, there is a little settlement called Qasigiannguit that is a hidden treasure just waiting to be discovered. The village of Qasigiannguit, whose name means "small bay" in the local tongue, is a wonderful location to explore because of the gorgeous fjords and mountains that surround it.

You'll notice Qasigiannguit's serene and tranquil ambience as soon as you get there. Even though it's tiny, there are lots of things to do here, including outdoor pursuits like hiking, fishing, and kayaking. You may visit the neighborhood museum to learn about the history and culture of the region or take a walk along the waterfront and take in the breathtaking views of the fjords and mountains.

You're in for a treat at Qasigiannguit if you love food. The area is also known for its mouthwatering seafood, which includes local fresh crab, shrimp, and halibut. These delicacies are available for tasting at one of the neighborhood eateries, or if you're feeling very daring, you may even try making them yourself.

The chance to see the local Inuits' traditional way of life is one of the pleasures of a trip to Qasigiannguit. You may take part in a cultural tour to discover more about their practices, convictions, and way of life. Also, you'll have the opportunity to engage in traditional Inuit pursuits like dog sledding and ice fishing.

Visit the community hall of the town in the evening to take in a distinctive sort of entertainment, a traditional Inuit drum dance. These dances, which are accompanied by music and storytelling, provide a window into the region's rich cultural legacy.

Qasigiannguit is a little, endearing village that provides tourists with a genuinely exceptional and immersive experience. There is something for everyone in this undiscovered treasure of Greenland, from its magnificent beauty to its rich cultural legacy.

Uummannaq

Another little island in northwest Greenland, Uummannaq is a jewel just waiting to be discovered. Uummannaq is the ideal location for anyone looking to escape the bustle of city life and immerse themselves in the beauty of nature thanks to its breathtaking landscape, rich cultural history, and welcoming local people.

The stunning beauty of Uummannaq is what draws most tourists there. Towering mountains, glittering glaciers, and pristine fjords may all be seen on the island from a variety of beautiful hiking paths. You may also take a boat trip of the fjords to see whales, seals, and other marine life while taking in the natural beauty of the island in a more leisurely manner.

Uummannaq has a beautiful landscape in addition to a rich cultural history. A robust Inuit population, which has been present on the island for many generations and has created a distinctive culture and way of life that is closely entwined with the land and the sea, resides there.

Visit the Uummannaq Museum, which features the history, art, and customs of the local Inuit people, to discover more about this rich cultural legacy.

Uummannaq is the ideal location if you want to experience the real Arctic. Visitors are invited to take part in customary pastimes like fishing, hunting, and dog sledding since the locals are so kind and hospitable.

In a manner that is impossible in more developed places, these encounters provide a unique chance to understand Inuit culture and establish connections with the land and the sea.

Lastly, it's crucial to remember that Uummannaq is situated in one of the wildest and most isolated regions on earth. This implies that travelers should be ready to live simply and sustainably and should be prepared for the harsh Arctic climate.

Yet Uummannaq is a memorable place that is well worth the effort because of its beautiful environment, rich cultural history, and welcoming locals.

Sermiligaaq

In Greenland's north, there lies a tiny, isolated settlement called Sermiligaaq. A unique and interesting fusion of the local culture and the Arctic's natural splendor may be found there. Sermiligaaq welcomes visitors and is a paradise for nature lovers, animal watchers, and anybody interested in seeing a genuine Inuit settlement.

Arriving at Sermiligaaq, tourists are immediately struck by the area's breathtaking surroundings. Rugged, snow-capped mountains, undulating hills, and pristine lakes around the hamlet. Visitors have the opportunity to go on a guided trek to explore the area's breathtaking glaciers up close. This is an opportunity of a lifetime that shouldn't be passed up!

Visitors to Sermiligaaq are also attracted in large part by the local culture. This is one of the few locations in the globe where tourists may see how the Inuit live traditionally. Visitors are welcome to participate in a hunting expedition or try their hand at fishing. Subsistence hunting and fishing are still practiced by the locals of Sermiligaaq. There is a nearby school in the area where guests may watch classes and engage with the pupils.

A wildlife viewing expedition is one of the greatest ways to explore Sermiligaaq's culture and animals. Many Arctic animals, including reindeer, Arctic foxes, and even polar bears, may be seen in the region. Participate on a guided tour to observe these incredible animals in their natural environment.

For anyone seeking to get away from the rush and bustle of contemporary life and experience something really unique and genuine culturally, Sermiligaaq is a must-visit location. There is something for everyone in this isolated region of Greenland, from the breathtaking landscape to the native culture and fauna.

Kangilinnguit

A little settlement called Kangilinnguit is found in Greenland's north. This village, which has a population of around 1,200, is tranquil and welcoming to tourists and guests. Kangilinnguit is the ideal location for you if you're searching for a distinctive cultural experience and a chance to escape the stress of city life.

The community museum in Kangilinnguit, which presents the history and culture of the Inuit people, is one of the city's top attractions. You may discover more about the traditional way of life, including hunting, fishing, and day-to-day living in the arid North here.

Also, you may see one-of-a-kind antiques and artworks that provide a window into the region's rich cultural legacy.

The breathtaking natural beauty of the region is another must-see in Kangilinnguit. Here is the ideal location to get lost in nature and appreciate the genuine beauty of the Arctic with its wide, pristine landscapes, steep mountain ranges, and crystal-clear lakes. There are activities for everyone here, whether you choose to walk, fish, or just soak in the gorgeous vistas.

Spending time with the nearby Inuit community is one of the greatest ways to experience Kangilinnguit. Here, you may experience a piece of the local way of life and discover their traditions and beliefs.

There are numerous possibilities to engage with the locals and fully immerse oneself in the culture, from eating regional specialties like Arctic char and reindeer meat to taking part in traditions like dog sledding and ice fishing.

For anybody seeking a cultural experience and a break from the routine, Kangilinnguit is an unique and intriguing place.

Qeqertarsuaq

The picturesque village of Qeqertarsuaq, commonly called Disko Island, is situated in the center of Greenland. This little village, which has just over 1,000 residents, gives tourists the opportunity to experience local culture and take in Greenland's natural splendor.

The beautiful scenery that surrounds the town of Qeqertarsuaq will astound visitors. The region is a haven for nature lovers, with its undulating hills, glaciers, and fjords. You may either trek the adjacent hills for expansive views of the surrounding landscapes or take a stroll along the coastline and watch the ice floes flow past.

Kayaking and ice fishing are popular sports that provide thrill-seekers the opportunity to genuinely feel the Arctic's untamed majesty.

The Disko Island Museum is located in the town and offers information about the Inuit history and culture. With displays showing the local Inuit way of life, including their hunting and fishing skills and cultural customs, the museum provides a captivating and participatory experience.

Qeqertarsuaq is the ideal location to buy a special and significant souvenir to remember your vacation since it has several local businesses offering traditional Inuit handicrafts.

There are many cultural activities available for anyone looking for a fully comprehensive experience. Visitors get the chance to take a step back in time and experience life as it was for the native inhabitants of the Arctic via activities like dog sledding, ice fishing, and traditional Inuit dances.

Qeqertarsuaq is the ideal location, whether you're looking for adventure or a chance to take it easy and enjoy the little things in life.

Tasiilaq

Little village Tasiilaq is situated in the eastern region of Greenland and is encircled by breathtaking glaciers and snow-covered mountains. The biggest community in the Ammassalik district, this lively town is home to over 2,000 people.

Tasiilaq is a great place for tourists to go if they enjoy outdoor activity and want to see the unadulterated beauty of nature. The surroundings of the town are stunning. It serves as a center for outdoor pursuits including kayaking, fishing, hiking, and whale watching.

The magnificent Sermilik Fjord, a top spot for fishing and kayaking, is one of Tasiilaq's features. This lovely fjord is encircled by tall mountains and is a well-liked tourist attraction.

Visitors may enjoy the excitement of kayaking across the fjord's frigid waters and catching some of the freshest fish in the world with the proper gear and guide.

Hiking is another well-liked pastime in Tasiilaq. A number of well-known routes that lead to glaciers, mountains, and other breathtaking natural beauties are accessible from the town. There is a path for every level of expertise, whether you are an expert hiker or just getting started.

Tasiilaq has a long history and is home to a number of museums that highlight the regional Inuit culture and traditions, making it a great destination for cultural enthusiasts. Via exhibitions and guided tours, visitors may learn about the region's history and the traditional way of life of the Inuit people.

Last but not least, Tasiilaq is a fantastic place to go whale watching. A number of different kinds of whales may be seen in the region where the town is located, which is well recognized for its variety of marine life. Joining a whale watching cruise will allow visitors to observe these majestic animals up close.

For people who like the outdoors, adventure, and culture, Tasiilaq is a must-visit location.

Upernavik

Beautiful fjords, glaciers, and ice-covered mountains surround the picturesque town of Upernavik in northwest Greenland. This town is ideal for tourists seeking adventure since it provides a variety of activities including kayaking, fishing, and hiking.

One of the most northern communities in the world, the town is home to around 1000 people. Despite being so far away, the people of Upernavik are exceedingly kind and will go out of their way to make sure you have a wonderful day.

They are deeply rooted in their way of life and are proud of their Inuit history, which they are glad to share with outsiders.

Kayaking is one of the most thrilling things to do in Upernavik. You may experience some of the most stunning landscapes in the world when kayaking in the fjords and canals that surround the town. You will undoubtedly have a blast whether you are a seasoned kayaker or a beginner.

Another well-liked activity in Upernavik is fishing, which tourists may do on their own or as part of one of the numerous fishing cruises. You may expect to catch a variety of fish, including Arctic char and halibut, since the town is close to some of Greenland's top fishing locations.

There are a number of hiking paths that may lead trekkers to some of the most stunning and inaccessible regions of Greenland. Beautiful glaciers, ice-covered mountains, and amazing animals will all be visible to you.

For tourists seeking adventure, Upernavik is a must-visit location. The town is surrounded by breathtaking natural beauty, and its inhabitants are kind and inviting.

Paamiut

The quaint and serene village of Paamiut, sometimes called Frederikshb, is situated on Greenland's southwest coast. This little fishing community is surrounded by breathtaking fjords and undulating hills, giving it the ideal location for tourists looking for a distinctive and authentic experience in Greenland.

The following are some things visitors to Paamiut should be aware of:

Nature: The town is bordered by some of Greenland's most breathtaking natural features, like towering cliffs, narrow fjords, and undulating hills. During a boat excursion, tourists may see the stunning coastline and stop at surrounding islands to look for seals, whales, and eagles.

Culture: Paamiut is a historic and culturally diverse town. By visiting the neighborhood museum, visitors may learn about the Inuit culture and traditions while seeing historical artifacts, attire, and hunting equipment. The community also has a thriving cultural hub where guests may take part in seminars and other activities.

Food: The fresh, delectable fish meals served at local eateries in Paamiut, which are known for their seafood, are available to tourists. Reindeer, seal, and whale meat are traditional meals in Greenland and are also used in many recipes.

Activities: The town is a fantastic starting point for outdoor pursuits including kayaking, fishing, and hunting. Also, tourists may go whale watching or enjoy a lovely drive along the shore.

Paamiut offers a variety of lodging choices, such as hotels, bed & breakfasts, and guesthouses. Depending on their interests and money, visitors may choose anything from simple to opulent solutions.

In general, Paamiut is the ideal location for tourists who wish to experience Greenland's distinctive culture and natural beauty. Visitors will discover a kind and inviting community in Paamiut, which offers a peaceful getaway from the bustle of daily life.

CHAPTER 5

FOOD AND DRINK

Cuisine in Greenland

The northern hemisphere country of Greenland is well known for its distinct and delectable food, which is a reflection of both its untamed natural environment and its rich cultural legacy. Fresh seafood is a staple of the nation's culinary scene and is eaten in a number of ways, including grilled, boiled, steamed, or raw, thanks to its clear seas. Suaasat, kiviak, and mattak are a few of the most well-liked traditional foods.

Suaasat

Greenland's traditional cuisine, suaasat, highlights the distinctive ingredients and tastes of the area. It is a traditional meal that has been handed down through the years and is ingrained in Greenland culture. Seal flesh is simmered in a broth with bay leaves, onions, potatoes, and other vegetables and herbs to create suaasat.

Suaasat is a dish that visitors to Greenland really must experience. The seal flesh is juicy and soft, and the broth is thick, aromatic, and delicious. It is the ideal way to sample local cuisine and enjoy Greenland's distinctive tastes.

Suaasat is a common menu item at many Greenlandic eateries, where it's often ordered as a soup or a main course. The chance to sample this classic cuisine in a fun setting is also often provided at regional festivals and events.

Suaasat is definitely a meal to try when in Greenland if you like robust, flavorful foods. It is a genuine and scrumptious method to sample the distinctive tastes of the area and to get fully immersed in local culture. So while visiting Greenland, be sure to include Suaasat on your gastronomic agenda.

Seafood

You're in for a treat when it comes to seafood if you're visiting or traveling through Greenland. The Arctic Ocean surrounds the nation, giving it the ideal location to savor delectable fish delicacies. Greenland's cuisine won't let you down whether you love fish or are simply seeking to try something different.

One of the most popular seafood meals in Greenland is fish soup, which is prepared using a variety of fish, including halibut, cod, and salmon. Bay leaves, pepper, and lemon are used to season the soup, giving it a distinctive flavor. This meal is available in the majority of eateries and coffee shops around the nation.

Kippefisk, a dish consisting of dried cod and haddock that is also quite popular, is another well-known meal. This meal is a standard fare in many Greenlandic homes and is often served with bread and butter.

Try mattak, a raw, marinated fish, for a more daring seafood experience. In Greenland, mattak, which is manufactured from whale skin and fat, is prized as a delicacy. It has a strong, unique taste and a chewy texture.

At some of Greenland's more contemporary restaurants, you may enjoy seafood-based fusion cuisine in addition to the traditional fish dishes. In order to give these recipes a distinctive and delectable touch, local items often used in them include reindeer meat and Arctic berries.

Don't forget to sample some of the fish delicacies when you visit Greenland. The native cuisine has a rich cultural heritage that is well worth researching, and the fish is always freshly caught.

Native Ingredients

Expect to be tantalized by the distinctive tastes and ingredients utilized in the native cuisine while visiting Greenland. These are a few of the regional foods that tourists may expect to find when visiting Greenland.

Meat from seals is a common element and a delicacy in Greenlandic cooking. It may be grilled, boiled, dried, or used in soups and stews. It can even be served as the main course.

Cod liver oil is a mainstay of Greenlandic cooking and is utilized for both its health advantages and to flavor food.

Because of its high vitamin A and D content, it is often added to stews, soups, and other foods to improve their taste.

Reindeer meat is a popular protein source in Greenland and is often prepared as a main course, either roasted or grilled. It is a favorite among both residents and tourists because of its flavorful and soft texture.

Arctic Char is a fish that may be found in Greenland's chilly seas and is often grilled or baked. It is regarded as a healthy alternative for people searching for a source of low-fat protein since it is high in omega-3 fatty acids.

Kelp is a seaweed that is often used in soups and salads and is found in large quantities in the seas around Greenland. Iodine, iron, and other crucial vitamins and minerals are abundant in it.

Berries - Berries are widely available in Greenland and are used in a wide range of recipes. Examples include blueberries, cranberries, and cloudberries. They are often used to produce jams, jellies, and syrups, as well as to flavor ice cream and other sweets.

Mussels and clams are two examples of shellfish that are often utilized in Greenlandic cooking. Usually eaten as a major meal or as an ingredient in soups and stews, they are boiled or steamed.

Several distinctive items may be found in Greenland that are employed in the native cuisine.

Eating Out in Greenland

Travelers and tourists may enjoy a unique and varied selection of food options in Greenland. You can find something to fit your taste whether you're searching for a sit-down restaurant or a fast snack on the move.

Places to eat in Greenland

If you're searching for a sit-down meal in Greenland, there are several restaurants that provide both traditional Inuit food and food with influences from other cultures. Popular eateries in the capital city of Nuuk include Kitchen & Table, which offers a variety of foreign and regional cuisine, and Kalaallit Nunaat, which specializes in traditional Inuit foods including seal meat.

Suaasat, an Inuit stew cooked with seal meat, potatoes, carrots, and other ingredients, is one of the must-try foods in Greenland. Reindeer steak, another well-liked delicacy, is offered at many eateries around the nation. Try the dried fish, a mainstay of the Inuit cuisine and often served as a side dish, if you're feeling daring.

International food, including pizza, sushi, and burgers, is available on the menu in addition to traditional meals. Also, many eateries include vegetarian and gluten-free alternatives, making it simple for those with dietary needs to locate food.

Cafes

In Greenland, cafes have a warm, welcoming environment that makes them ideal stops for a quick snack or cup of coffee.

Numerous cafés offer traditional Inuit delicacies made from caribou or musk ox wool, such as bannock bread and qiviut muffins. Together with a selection of teas, they also sell specialized coffee beverages including lattes and cappuccinos.

Be sure to start up a discussion with the locals to learn more about the culture and way of life in Greenland because cafes are a common place for residents to congregate and catch up with friends.

Greenland's markets for food

Travelers may try traditional Inuit dishes, as well as fresh vegetables and other locally sourced goods, at food markets in Greenland, which provide a distinctive and genuine experience. Certain markets, like the Nuuk Market, provide culinary demos where you may pick up a new recipe and skill to try at home while learning how to create traditional meals like suaasat.

You may get traditional Inuit foods including dried fish, caribou jerky, and Arctic char at Greenland's food shops. It's a terrific location to buy presents for friends and family back home since you can also get locally produced goods, such handcrafted crafts and souvenirs.

For tourists and travelers, dining out in Greenland provides a unique and unforgettable experience. There is something for everyone, from authentic Inuit food to worldwide cuisine, making it a must-visit location for foodies.

Drinking in Greenland

The frigid vistas of Greenland combine with warm friendliness in this region of contrasts. This disparity is also reflected in the food and beverages in this nation. Everyone may find something to enjoy in Greenland, from warm cups of coffee to locally created beverages.

Bars and Clubs

In Greenland, bars and clubs are fantastic places to meet people and relax after a day of seeing the stunning surroundings. There are a number of well-known pubs and clubs in the capital city of Nuuk, including the Qajaq Bar and Club, which is renowned for its energetic ambiance and live music.

Another well-liked location is Café Mandag, which provides delectable meals along with a selection of beers, wines, and drinks.

Greenland's food and drink are an essential component of its culture. In this incredible nation, there is something for everyone, whether you favor beer, wine, coffee, or tea. As a result, while traveling to Greenland, be sure to sample some native libations and take advantage of the friendly atmosphere there.

CHAPTER 6

PRACTICAL INFORMATION

Health and Safety

In order to enjoy your vacation to Greenland the most, it is crucial to be informed of the health and safety issues there.

When visiting Greenland, you need to understand Greenland's climate, which may be harsh and difficult, particularly for those who aren't acclimated to the country's bitter cold and wind. It is vital to dress in warm and waterproof clothes, including gloves, caps, and boots, since the nation has long, gloomy winters with temperatures that may dip far below zero.

Food safety is a problem in Greenland as well since many of the local delicacies, such fish and game, might contain contaminants or parasites. Guests are urged to stay away from raw or undercooked seafood and to stick to well-cooked and well-prepared foods. It's also important to be aware of infections that are transmitted by food and water and to take the necessary measures, such as drinking bottled water or avoiding raw meat.

Greenland has a modest but well-resourced healthcare system, with a limited number of hospitals and clinics. Nonetheless, it's crucial to pack a complete first aid kit and be ready for emergencies, particularly if you're going somewhere isolated. Visitors are also encouraged to bring a supply of any prescription drugs they may need and to be up to date on their immunizations.

Lastly, it's critical to be knowledgeable about the dangers posed by outdoor activities like hiking, kayaking, and fishing. With its rocky, steep mountains, glaciers, and fjords, Greenland's terrain may be difficult, so it's important to be equipped with the correct tools and to know your limitations.

You must be aware of the threats posed by animals, including polar bears and Arctic foxes, and take the necessary procedures to mitigate them.

Greenland is a fascinating and distinctive location that offers a plethora of options for exploration and adventure.

To truly enjoy your vacation and take advantage of everything that Greenland has to offer, it's crucial to be informed of the health and safety issues in the nation and to take the necessary measures.

Insurance and Vaccinations

For anybody visiting Greenland, travel insurance and vaccines are crucial concerns. For the protection it may provide in the case of unplanned cancellations, trip interruptions, and medical crises, travel insurance is a need.

The advice given to visitors is to get comprehensive travel insurance that covers every part of their vacation, including medical costs, lost baggage, and flight cancellations.

It is crucial to have all standard immunizations, including those for measles, mumps, rubella, and polio, as well as any extra immunizations that may be advised for travel to Greenland, including those for hepatitis A, hepatitis B, and rabies. For the most recent immunization advice, travelers are recommended to speak with a healthcare professional or travel clinic.

You must be aware of any possible health hazards related to Greenland's climate and environment, such as exposure to low temperatures and wind as well as diseases transmitted via food and water. Visitors are urged to exercise proper care, such as drinking only bottled water and avoiding raw meat, as well as to be ready for emergencies, particularly if they want to go to isolated locations.

To ensure a safe and pleasurable vacation, travelers to Greenland should take into account the need for travel insurance and immunizations. Guests are urged to make preparations and seek the most recent guidelines and guidance from a healthcare professional or travel clinic.

Crime and Safety Tips

With minimal safety issues for visitors and low levels of crime, Greenland is usually regarded as a safe place. To protect your safety, it's crucial to be informed of possible threats as with any trip place and to take the necessary safety measures.

Knowing the risks posed by the severe and unpredictable weather in Greenland is one of the most crucial safety advice, particularly in the winter when temperatures may plummet far below zero and high winds can produce blizzard-like conditions.

Visitors are encouraged to bring gloves, caps, and boots, as well as warm, waterproof clothes, and to be ready for emergencies, particularly if they want to go to isolated places.

Greenland is a reasonably secure location in terms of crime, with low incidences of theft and robbery. Visitors are cautioned to be watchful and take security measures to safeguard their personal property, such as locking up valuables and avoiding carrying significant quantities of cash.

It's also critical to be aware of the dangers that come with outdoor pursuits like hiking, kayaking, and fishing and to take the necessary steps to reduce those dangers. The necessary equipment, such as a GPS unit or a personal location beacon, and being aware of one's limitations are suggested for visitors before engaging in these activities.

Last but not least, it is suggested that tourists understand the hazards connected with animals, such as polar bears and

Arctic foxes, and take the necessary procedures to mitigate these risks. It is urged that visitors stay on well-traveled trails and steer clear of places where animals are known to be present.

With minimal safety issues and low levels of crime, Greenland is typically a safe place to visit. To protect your safety, it is crucial to be aware of possible hazards and to take the necessary measures, particularly while engaging in outdoor activities or visiting distant locations.

In order to safeguard their personal property and guarantee a secure and happy journey, you must be watchful and take meticulous steps.

Money and Payments

Visitors to Greenland will need to convert their money into this currency in order to make purchases and pay for services while they are there. Greenland utilizes the Danish Krone (DKK) as its official currency.

Using ATMs, which are extensively accessible in the main cities and towns, including the capital city of Nuuk, is the simplest and most practical option to convert money.

Before traveling, customers are urged to check with their bank or credit card company to make sure their card will be accepted and to learn about any costs that may apply.

In Greenland, credit cards and debit cards are widely accepted and provide a quick and secure method to make payments for goods and services. The most widely used credit cards are Visa, Mastercard, and American Express. Visitors are recommended to contact their card issuer in advance of their travel to ensure that their card will be accepted and to learn about any fees that may apply.

Be aware of the fees involved with using credit cards and ATMs in Greenland since they may rapidly mount, particularly if you use them often. Guests are urged to confirm any applicable costs before their journey by contacting their bank or credit card provider.

Cash is still a popular form of payment in Greenland, particularly in more rural and small-town regions, and it remains a practical means to make purchases and pay for services. It is suggested that visitors bring along enough small-denomination currency to cover any eventualities when credit cards or ATMs are not accessible.

In order to make purchases and pay for services when traveling to Greenland, travelers will need to convert their cash into Danish Krone (DKK). While credit cards, debit cards, and ATMs are commonly accepted in Greenland, travelers are encouraged to be mindful of the fees associated with using these payment methods and to carry enough small denomination currency.

Currency Exchange

For tourists to Greenland who need to transfer their money into the country's official currency, the Danish Krone, currency exchange is a vital step (DKK). Banks, currency exchange shops, and ATMs are only a few of the possibilities for currency conversion.

Banks are an easy way to convert money since they provide reasonable exchange rates and are extensively present throughout Greenland's main cities and villages, including the capital city of Nuuk. Nevertheless, banks could only be open during certain hours, and there might be a delay while exchanging money.

Tourists are urged to confirm any costs before their journey by contacting their bank.

Another alternative for currency conversion is a currency exchange bureau, which is commonly accessible throughout Greenland's main cities and villages, including the capital city of Nuuk.

Banks are closed less often than currency exchange offices, which makes them a handy choice for travelers. Visitors are recommended to evaluate conversion rates and costs across different currency exchange bureaus, nevertheless, since these factors might vary widely.

For travelers who need to withdraw money quickly, Greenland's ATMs offer a practical and extensively used choice for currency conversion. In the main cities and towns, including the capital city of Nuuk, ATMs are extensively accessible and provide favorable exchange rates.

In Greenland, there are several places to convert money, including banks, bureaus of exchange, and ATMs.

Tipping Customs

Greenland's tipping traditions are comparable to those in other Western nations. While leaving a tip is not required, it is customary to do so to express gratitude for excellent service.

10% of the entire cost is often left as a tip at restaurants, however this might change based on how well the service was provided. It's customary to leave modest cash or a few kroner as a tip at cafés and pubs.

It's customary to give hotel cleaning employees a few kroner as a tip each day, however the amount might change based on how well the service was provided.

While the drivers of cabs don't demand tips, it is customary to round up the fare to the closest krone as a sign of gratitude.

Greenland's tipping traditions are comparable to those in other Western nations, and it is customary to give a modest tip to express gratitude for excellent service at restaurants, cafés and bars, hotels, and taxis.

CHAPTER 7

ADDITIONAL INFORMATION

Local Events and Festivals

Travelers and tourists from all over the globe like visiting Greenland because of its rich culture and traditions. In Greenland, there is something for everyone, whether you want to learn about the local Inuit culture or participate in cultural and athletic activities. Below is a detailed list of all the regional celebrations and events you may attend in Greenland.

Inuit Customary Holidays

For thousands of years, the Inuit people have resided in Greenland, and their culture and customs are still very much present today. The Summer Festival, also known as Nalunnguat, which occurs in June, is one of the most important events in the Inuit calendar.

The Inuit people gather to celebrate the start of summer and the return of the sun after a protracted, gloomy winter at this event.

Traditional games, drum dance, eating, and other events and activities all take place throughout the celebration. Families and communities gather at this time to celebrate one another, and guests are always invited to take part in the festivities.

Sports and Culture Events

Many athletic and cultural activities take place in Greenland and are accessible to tourists. The Arctic Sounds Music Festival, which takes place in the village of Sisimiut in July, is one of the most well-liked occasions. In addition to traditional Inuit drumming and dance, this event showcases a wide variety of regional and worldwide musical artists.

The Arctic Cultural Festival, which takes place in the town of Nuuk in August, is another cultural event not to be missed. This event features displays of indigenous goods, music, and dancing that highlight the Inuit people's rich cultural legacy.

The Arctic Circle Race is a must-see event for sports aficionados. This cross-country ski competition, which takes place in the village of Sisimiut, is one of the most challenging ones ever. This event is an actual test of strength and endurance due to the stunning scenery and difficult terrain.

Festivals of Dance and Music

In Greenland, there are many festivals that honor these customs since music and dancing are central to Inuit culture. The Nuuk Nordic Cultural Festival, which takes place in the capital city of Nuuk in August, is one of the most well-known music events.

This festival offers a variety of musical acts, including both modern folk and pop music and traditional Inuit music.

The Arctic Sounds Festival, which takes place in the town of Sisimiut in July, is another music event not to be missed. Arctic music and culture are celebrated during this event, which features both domestic and foreign performers.

The Arctic Dance Festival is a must-attend event for dance enthusiasts. A variety of traditional Inuit dances are performed as part of this festival, which takes place in the town of Nuuk in August. Visitors may participate in seminars and lessons, as well as learn about the many forms of Inuit dancing.

In Greenland, there is something for everyone, whether you want to learn about the local Inuit culture or participate in cultural and athletic activities.

Sustainable and Responsible Travel

Travelers looking for a distinctive, action-packed experience in a pure, natural setting may consider visiting Greenland. Yet, the expansion of tourism has the potential to have an adverse effect on both the indigenous inhabitants' way of life and the vulnerable Arctic ecology. For this reason, it is crucial for visitors to Greenland to travel sustainably and responsibly.

Sustainable travel is maximizing the positive effects of tourism while limiting its negative effects on the environment and local populations. To ensure that the people, animals, and environment of Greenland endure for many more years, respect is a need. These are a few things visitors to Greenland can do to travel sustainably:

To cut down on transportation-related carbon emissions, use public transit or sign up for a tour that uses sustainable techniques.

Consider staying in eco-friendly lodges or traditional Inuit accommodations, which place an emphasis on environmental preservation and assist local communities.

Bring reusable water bottles, steer clear of single-use plastics, and dispose of garbage correctly to reduce the amount of plastic waste that you make.

By consuming locally produced goods and patronizing neighborhood eateries and stores, you can show your support for the community.

Respect animals and their surroundings by keeping a safe distance from them and refraining from interfering with their normal activities.

Respect for Local Cultures and Wildlife

In addition to having a distinctive and varied culture, Greenland also has a wide variety of fauna. While traveling to Greenland, it's important to show respect for the indigenous people's customs and the animals, since both contribute significantly to the scenery and overall experience of this amazing nation.

Learn about the practices and traditions of the Inuit people, who make up the majority of Greenland's population, in order to show respect for the community's culture. This may be accomplished through going to cultural venues, taking part in customary pursuits, and conversing with locals.

By adhering to the rules for ethical wildlife watching, such as maintaining a safe distance from animals, not leaving trash in wildlife habitats, and not disrupting nests or habitats, you may prevent exploiting wildlife.

While engaging in outdoor activities, show respect for the environment by avoiding trash, destroying plants, and leaving no trace.

Emergency Contacts

Always be ready for crises and know how to get in touch with emergency services if you ever need them. Below is detailed advice for tourists and travelers on how to get in touch with Greenland's emergency services.

Emergency Contacts

Knowing the local emergency numbers is crucial in the event of an emergency. The emergency number in Greenland is 112, which is accessible from any phone, including mobile phones. By dialing this number, you may reach the police, fire department, and ambulance services as well as other emergency services. Never forget to dial 112 in case of emergency.

Clinics and Hospitals

There are a number of hospitals and clinics spread throughout the cities and villages of Greenland. The Queen Ingrid's Hospital, which provides medical services in all specialties including surgery, neurology, and cardiology, is the primary hospital in the capital city of Nuuk. It's a good idea to have a first aid kit and any essential medications with you if you're visiting isolated parts of Greenland.

Embassy and Consulates

You may get in touch with the closest embassy or consulate if you want consular help or have any other problems while visiting Greenland. Greenland is under the authority of the Danish Embassy in Washington, D.C., and there are other consulates spread out over the nation. Consulates and Embassies may be contacted through their websites or by calling the local tourism bureau in your area.

It's always wiser to travel safely than regrettably. If you need help, don't hesitate to call the closest consulate or embassy; just make sure you are acquainted with the emergency numbers and medical facilities in the region you are visiting.

Tips for a Successful Trip

The biggest island in the world, Greenland, is an unique and intriguing destination for tourists. Greenland provides a unique experience with its unspoiled wildness, spectacular scenery, and rich cultural history. Here are some suggestions for travelers to bear in mind in order to assist them have a successful and enjoyable vacation to Greenland.

Make a plan: Due to the fact that Greenland is not a conventional tourist destination, there is a little more planning and preparation needed. Before going, be sure to do some research on the activities, lodging, and transportation you want to use. Consider your visit's scheduling as well since some areas and attractions could not be accessible at certain periods of the year owing to weather.

Pack appropriately: The severe climate of Greenland has year-round lows of -40°C and highs of 10°C. So, it is crucial to carry warm, water-resistant apparel as well as strong shoes. Bring a hat, gloves, and sunglasses as well to protect yourself from the wind and the sun.

Respect the Environment: While visiting Greenland, it is essential to protect the ecology since it is special and delicate. Follow the Leave No Trace guidelines, which include not plucking wildflowers, properly disposing of waste, and not disturbing animals.

Learn About the Culture: Tourists are urged to become familiar with and respectful of Greenland's rich cultural history. Try the local cuisine, visit the local museums and cultural institutions, and strike up a discussion with the people. This is a fantastic opportunity to learn more about and appreciate the distinctive culture and customs of Greenland.

Accept Adventure: Greenland is a paradise for outdoor lovers and those looking for adventure. There is something for everyone, from kayaking and hiking to ice climbing and dog sledding. Profit from these chances and welcome the journey.

Be Safe: For those unfamiliar with the region, Greenland's vast wilderness may be deadly. While participating in outdoor activities, be careful to follow the required safety measures, notify someone of your intentions, and carry a GPS gadget.

Appreciate the Beauty: With spectacular scenery and amazing natural treasures, Greenland is a visually attractive vacation. Take some time to pause and take in this wonderful place's breathtaking beauty.

Choose the Correct Season: The weather in Greenland may change dramatically throughout the year and is erratic. The finest weather for outdoor activities is during the summer months, while dog sledding and seeing the Northern Lights are best done in the winter. Depending on the activities you want to do, choose the appropriate season.

Consider Hiring a Local Guide: To assist you discover the wild areas of Greenland, think about hiring a local guide. They will not only guarantee your safety and assist you in navigating the sometimes difficult terrain, but they will also provide you insightful information about the region's history and culture.

Sample the Local Cuisine: Tourists are urged to sample the distinctive and delectable food of Greenland. Locally cultivated vegetables and fruit are used with fish, seal, and whale meat in traditional meals. This is a fantastic opportunity to get a taste of the regional customs and food.

Be Weather-Ready: The weather in Greenland is unpredictable, so travelers should be ready for everything. To make sure you are comfortable and safe throughout your vacation, pack a lot of warm clothes, a waterproof jacket, and sturdy shoes.

Visitors may have an absolutely amazing experience by taking the time to explore and enjoy Greenland and by using the advice in this section.

CONCLUSION

Greenland is a breathtaking location that provides tourists with a unique fusion of natural beauty, native culture, and contemporary conveniences. Travelers looking for an unforgettable experience, nature lovers, and adventurers will all like this distant island country.

Greenland is a great place to go whether you're an experienced traveler or simply seeking a memorable holiday. We've covered all the must-see attractions, must-do activities, and must-try cuisine in this guide. Also, we've included pointers and suggestions on how to organize your vacation, what to bring, and how to get about.

For those seeking some peace and quiet and a place to get away from the throng, Greenland is a fantastic option. Visitors will feel as if they have entered a foreign universe because of the area's huge, open landscapes and low population density.

Greenland is a must-see location, regardless of whether you're traveling alone, with a partner, or with your family.

Greenland is a special place with a memorable experience for everyone. There are many possibilities to discover and take in the finest that this magnificent nation has to offer, whether you're a nature lover, an adventurer, or a culture vulture. So prepare for an adventure by packing your luggage, and then go traveling!

TRAVEL

DATE:

DURATION:

DESTINATION:

PLACES TO SEE:	LOCAL FOOD TO TRY:
1	1
2	2
3	3
4	4
5	5
6	6
7	7

DAY 1	DAY 2	DAY 3

DAY 4	DAY 5	DAY 6

NOTES	EXPENSES IN TOTAL:

PLANNER

TRAVEL

DATE:

DURATION:

DESTINATION:

PLACES TO SEE:	LOCAL FOOD TO TRY:
1	1
2	2
3	3
4	4
5	5
6	6
7	7

DAY 1	DAY 2	DAY 3

DAY 4	DAY 5	DAY 6

NOTES	EXPENSES IN TOTAL:

PLANNER

TRAVEL

DATE:

DURATION:

DESTINATION:

PLACES TO SEE:	LOCAL FOOD TO TRY:
1	1
2	2
3	3
4	4
5	5
6	6
7	7

DAY 1	DAY 2	DAY 3

DAY 4	DAY 5	DAY 6

NOTES	EXPENSES IN TOTAL:

PLANNER

TRAVEL

DATE:

DURATION:

DESTINATION:

PLACES TO SEE:	LOCAL FOOD TO TRY:
1	1
2	2
3	3
4	4
5	5
6	6
7	7

DAY 1	DAY 2	DAY 3

DAY 4	DAY 5	DAY 6

NOTES	EXPENSES IN TOTAL:

PLANNER

Made in the USA
Las Vegas, NV
03 August 2023

75603783R00075